I AM
the Messenger
MESSAGES OF LOVE TO STIR THE SOUL

MARYLIN FORBES

Prepared for publication by The Book Incubator, 2018
www.bookincubator.com.au
Bunbury, Western Australia

©Marylin Forbes, July 2018
Editor Karen Collyer
Cover photograph @Marylin Forbes
Photograph of author by Helen

Book layout and design The Book Incubator.
Soft Cover ISBN-13: 978-0-6481563-3-8
E-Book ISBN: 978-0-6481563-4-5

I AM THE LIGHT

I AM the Light of this World.

Join me – come to me and bathe in the Glory of the coming days. Give Joy to all wherever you can. Spring to life with the Godspring within all. Seek satisfaction in spreading Light. For I AM is with you all the way.

Seek out those who you trust. Work together and I will shine my Light and Love on Thee.

Tell them all not to fear for a new World will appear where all can share in purity and care. Uplift thine eyes to the central core – that brilliant shining light. See that all is well before the storm that clears the night.

Be sure of Thy footsteps along the way.

Use My Love

I'll see you there.

I AM the Messenger - Messages of Love to Stir the Soul is dedicated to Hermann Müller- a humble and loving gentleman who set the hearts of the world he touched on fire. He led a rich and fulfilled life quest of seeking what is pure in the hearts of men and women. His pupils adored him as he showed them how to inspire others to achieve heart, mind and spirit to become one; through awareness of the sacred geometry, facial and body reading that exposed the deep connection to the soul. Thousands were saddened by their loss of a genuine Earth master. His wife Marie, humbly carried Hermann's Excalibur Sword at his end.

Dear Reader,

Life can be a great tormentor, the great cyclic happenings that give us our ups and downs.

On reflecting on my many writings and heartfelt feelings and angelic messages, there are a number that stand apart. Messages in 2002/3 of my beginnings, and prior to that for that amazing introduction to the eventual gigantic, life-changing shift that settled on me in my early thirties.

These things I will enlighten you with through the touching, and sometimes heart wrenching communications, with the resulting life-tale that follows.

In 2005 words flowed and "Take Thy Brother's Hand" came through, humbling yet sustaining what I knew was already in my psyche, that is to be there and observe. How amazing that this popped up again when I was struggling where to begin amongst all the scripts that reflect Love of man and facets of despair as well.

Reading with more reflection of my Guide's words that my life will be protected and loved, I came across that which was completed on Easter Friday 2007, with the instruction for me to 'take up the cross and clear the way' with the first lines reading 'When the stars align with the planets...'

Another World upheaval began some years ago, justly illustrated by the outpouring of emotions over the untimely death of Princess Diana, and again the terrorist attacks of 9/11 in New York. I believe both events registered readings that flew off NASA instrumentation, indicating to me that the power of Love is real and accessible.

The synchronicity to the reflection 'stars aligning with planets' historical event, foretold by the Maya people and other highly knowledgeable entities, will bring about significant changes to Mother Earth and its people's higher consciousness; the express need for tuning into our higher selves amazing achievements obtained through Love.

In January that year my work 'Forward - My Walk With the WAY' began evolving into I Am the Messenger- Messages of Love to Stir the Soul, and explains my long journey to this current point in time. The Love from God guides and protects me.

I believe we must all get back to what we started with in life, Purity and Love. The Trust in the Holy Spirit who lives in us all, in our DNA, in our hearts, I now send to you.

Please read these messages as aspects of our very lives, the ups and downs we bear each day, our loves and our losses, so they may guide and offer the peace intended.

God's blessings meant for you.

Believe and Trust in the I AM that I AM always and you will be led in peace and contentment.

Ehyeh-asher-ehyeh

I AM that I AM

The messages contained in this companion work, "I Am the Messenger – Messages of Love to Stir the Soul" illustrate that our hearts and our guiding angels are there always, ready to assist by way of dreams and whispers, in this case prompting notations during the day or night.

This is what I give to you now... place your TRUST in the GOD SPIRIT who lives within YOU.

Ehyeh Asher Ehyeh

I give thanks to all those persons who have been

instrumental in forming the I AM of I AM.

May you also find what you
may be searching for.

With many blessings
Marylin
Amethyst Starchild

With the beautiful and extra-ordinary music playing to my heart and memories on the cold, wet miserable day that refreshed the parched earth came the realization that this is what I have been waiting for, a tangible beginning to something great. The time has arrived.

WHERE TO BEGIN...

Apart from dreams and exploring that given, I remember clearly sitting at peace on the veranda of my Mt Richon home in 2002.

The home was relatively new to me and overlooked Neerigen Brook and a swathe of mature bush. The softly falling rain on the eucalypt branches seemed to reach out for my hands.

I remember reading a booklet on Daniel and then the words just seemed to flow. It was a beginning. The Book of Daniel is a pivotal point of my spiritual journey and I have much gratitude for the guidance.

A weekend in August 2010 proved to be an extremely uplifting one. Flowering passion, love and wonderment of meeting high-minded souls whose passion in life is to guide others to comprehend just how huge and wonderful the love is for ourselves and the ability to achieve marvelous things available to us all. Our God self that surrounds us and yet lives within us, that is always there loving us and keeping us safe. The knowing exists for eternity.

My God self-made this book available to me without asking, ready for the long-promised journey ahead, to document for my children, grandchildren and their children, of my being and eventually, my going. Documenting the wondrous association with God and all things in what I call I Am the Messenger – Messages of Love to Stir the Soul.

I called on my highest self to assist me with the early memories. The help came, and recollected with love. After all, it is my life and precious to me.

To be able to return in a new life and maybe, just maybe, an understanding of what has occurred in this paragon of time would be interesting. The Time Shift, to the New Age we are now experiencing and a great force that is changing the World I know and understand. Let this be a record for all to preserve.

⚬❧ ⟞⟞ ⟞⟞ ☙⚬

I met my pack mother more than 50,000 years ago, from the il-E-Wari tribe. My own mother had passed away at the Great Oval Basin. She took care of me until I sustained myself. My name is Wonchita-Arie. I knew her as SHANTI-A—the noble one. 2003.

⚬❧ ⟞⟞ ⟞⟞ ☙⚬

TURNING POINT

There came a point in my life when I realised there must be something more... something in my life that would fill the void in my being.

I was yearning for the emptiness to disappear and make me feel ONE again. Little did I know how my life would change over the coming years.

As related by my dearly loved mother, I arrived with a rush, which is rather amusing considering that in this present life rushing around is not something I enjoy but tend to endure.

Life should be lived gently, yet earnestly. Some say that too quick a birth has its consequences as the slow arrival prepares one-self for the birthing process (rather like the silk worm that takes hours to free itself from its cocoon prison, the struggle so necessary for it to emerge strong and ready to fly).

However, not being a new Soul, this may not have been a requirement for me. How do I know that? This is what you can discover for yourself. Read, absorb and understand just how great, how lovely, the human experience with Spirit is.

Now is my time at last!

Thank you I AM.

For many women there comes a time shift where things seem different - not fulfilling, even though we love our families so much and our children are our delight. Yet there is a void. One is not quite sure of oneself - and just what is it?

Amazing is a term that lives with me always. The words of a tune that kept running around my mind was, "Is that all there is? Is that all there is my friend? Then let's keep dancing....," by the famous jazz singer Peggy Lee.

This song profoundly affected many thousands, if not millions of souls, for its absolute honesty. Many like-minded scholars and writers acknowledge this connection.

My journey started early, when my son was just four and my beautiful daughter was born after heartaches of losing wanted children for better or worse.

The years flowed by as they do, some good, some not so good and surviving some critical health situations on more than one occasion. The children had a life full of activities and the luxury of boating up and down our wonderful West Australian coastline and rivers, fully supported in sporting efforts and close family connections. Life in general appeared good, as a busy working mother, father on shift work, great friends and social occasions.

One significant event helped shaped my future life. How I remember this so clearly was the sheer fact that the landscape had changed where our family would collect fallen timber in the Darling Range near Jarrahdale for our tile fire.

This time there was utter devastation. Not a beautiful jarrah, banksia or flower left. Alcoa had come through the back of the beautiful Jarrahdale area with their machinery and cleared a massive swathe that left bare gravel. The remains of a huge king jarrah beside the wide area caught my eye and I stretched out my hand to touch the centre of the stump.

My heart bled for I felt it cry, "Why, oh why is this beautiful temple of God's creation and ancient age treated with such disrespect?"

My knowing is that such trees form part of the ley lines that circle the earth. Today, as a tree and free spirit, I respond and appreciate the same energy when viewing these magnificent creations.

HEARTACHE

During his late teenage years, our son became a total stranger through the influence of the boys he knew from kindergarten and unfortunate choices.

Our hearts were broken and felt beyond repair. His sister also suffered because the focus was now away from her own elite sporting activities that demanded our attention. It was a very sad time.

However, one of these friend's mother asked if I would like to go to church with her to see if it would help. The church was a local Baptist one with a visiting American firebrand preacher who belted out a sermon with passion.

My son was with me the night that God's glowing golden tear drops poured over the two of us - what a feeling! There is nothing on earth that can ever match being in the loving presence of God.

From then on, so many missionaries came to my home seeking discussion, or even requiring my secretarial services. Then a new client arrived, Charlie Cuff, and everything changed. Charlie worked with aboriginals building their homes in the far north of Western Australia. He was a lay preacher and his home fellowship became a pivotal point in my life, and to some degree with my eldest child as well.

On one fellowship evening, the group of seven were taking turns reading passages from The Book of Daniel. I remember so clearly reading verses on The Kings, and then having been abruptly torn away from focus by a massive gurgling wind that rooted me to the spot, it came from my very loins.

It roared from my mouth for what seemed to be an eternity. Charlie rushed over and began to bless me and from that moment an unlearned language and the ability of my hands to do marvelous work was implanted. It was the start of an incredible journey for me.

Not long after, my son came into my bedroom one evening to say that a force that he had never felt before had him on his knees in his own bedroom, something that felt so different to what his mind was experiencing at that time.

There was also the time when Reg, an elderly fellowship member in our small group, was slipping away with prostate cancer. Spirit would pick me up and take me to his bedside to pray in tongues that he seemed to understand.

Our family were spending available weekends at the Bridgetown shack. I loved its five hectares and rocky granite. At the time of Reg's illness in January 1996 I felt the need to climb to the block's highest point.

A magical force sent my arms out high to my sides and a voice erupting from within in what seemed to me as American Indian chanting with, "go and give comfort to those in need."

I panicked, thinking who? Is it my recently widowed Bridgetown neighbour, my son, or is it my accountant who suffers also? No.

Returning to our suburban home, the phone rang. Charlie had been desperately trying to contact me all weekend. Reg was dying in St John's Hospital Murdoch. So, on a rainy January day, witnessed by his wife, his son and Charles Cuff, Reg received his last rights through my gift of prayer. He passed away two hours later.

CHANGING DIRECTION WITH SPIRIT

The same night that Reg passed away I was again guided to the computer where my hands just flew to the beat of their own drum and recorded over several A4 pages my journey with this group of people. This ancient force was guiding me to say goodbye to the life that I had known for so long.

Residents of Western Australia will remember the terrible news of the first of what turned out to be serial murders, again in January of 1996. As mentioned previously, my life was experiencing great change. I can clearly remember, as if it were yesterday, hearing the news Sarah Spiers was missing. Immediately a voice boomed in my head, "she is dead."

Frantically I wrote down the next statement '2 2 Petry'. Anxiety sets in big time. What do I do?

I rang a client who had similar resonances with me, but she could only say to go with my gut. Then I decided that okay, it could be an address?

I searched our road map and sure enough there was a Petry Road, in Langford. Langford was an area renowned at that time for not being the best suburb to live in if you had a choice. It was also only a few kilometres from my Willetton home.

Leaving my husband in bewilderment, I took off on my search. Lo and behold there was no number 22. It was a very short street. To this day, I still have the flip calendar with that date and time and remarks.

What disturbs me so much is the fact alarm bells rang again when newspaper reports some years later related an unfortunate happening to a young Aboriginal male in that area.

I was relieved to hear of the Claremont serial killer's arrest on December 22, 2016.

His trial date = 22 years from this offence.

Re-occurring "22"

I discovered also that Petry = Death.

I often wonder what I have been dealt. How to deal with it? Another murder case of a young girl missing from Victoria Park for ages, and the authorities looking for a pale blue small sedan.

Feelings again? There was a pale blue vehicle right behind our property that never seemed to move! Right, girl your imagination is working overtime.

It took some time to register those feelings to the Police. Remembering angels do not necessarily work their stuff the same as we do. The registration was never acknowledged. Put it to rest.

So many instances where I have been called to those who are ready to pass on to another existence!

It was not long after that when life direction changed again to take my husband and I to buy and operate Riverwood House Bed and Breakfast/Restaurant in Bridgetown. Other stories suffice that affected me strongly, proved over, and over again to me how strong the Spirit is when something needs to be done for others.

One that did leave me smiling was when my mother's remaining brother, Frank, was seriously ill in Hollywood Hospital. After prayer in Frank's comatose presence for a safe passage, Mother and I ventured into the garden outside to find a group of visitors and a mosaic as a work in progress.

The work organiser invited our partaking in naming and placing tiles into the work, representing our family member. I immediately said to her with full knowing, "You have the name now, it is Ascending Souls." The work depicted a landscape of green fields with golden shards flowing towards the sun, intended for the Hollywood Hospital Chapel.

RIVERWOOD HOUSE

Getting to Riverwood House Bed & Breakfast/Restaurant had its own journey. Our family was experiencing Bridgetown on a part-time basis on five hectares in Walter Road, just outside of town.

We had converted an old, expansive wooden structure that had been used in early times as a packing shed. It was from there we began to look for a business so Bridgetown would be our permanent home.

Whilst there my husband and I woke one morning, each awakening from significant dreams. His vivid dream focused on him giving notice at The Swan Brewery. Mine was about seeing and walking into a beautiful yellow room that beckoned me!

Not long after my daughter and I were shopping at Garden City when we saw the famous artist Darryl Trott's 1995 artwork of 'Poppies' set in a golden frame.

It left me breathless.

"That is for my beautiful yellow room."

It remains a treasured possession, not only as a memory of my fiftieth birthday, but also of the grand home that would take one's breath away. The yellow room was Riverwood House's gorgeous foyer!

We eventually sold our own home to one of the owners of Riverwood House. We became its new caretakers for one never really owns such a property. Generation after generation have experienced this wonderful riverside property.

Not long after we had settled in, a strange experience had me feeling unsettled. What was that? Something felt like a soft wind brushing my shoulder?

I looked up from my computer and put down my account entries. My awareness had every hair standing to attention. This was something entirely new, a loving breathe-like sensation!

A phone call from my mother a few hours later revealed that my beloved Uncle Jack, her brother, had just passed away after a long illness. I've always had a very special place in my heart for this gentleman. He was instrumental in my safe arrival into this world and it seemed fitting that he be there for me in his departure.

His final blessing was the gentle wisp of wind felt on my shoulder. I look forward to having him on my family tree in whatever new life comes.

Riverwood House was renowned for its Devonshire teas, something that had me floundering because I had never had this experience. Scones, heaven help me! Help arrived in the form of a guest, a lovely Australian woman who lived in Oregon, USA!

Sensing the anguish, she gave me her sister's recipe that consequently sustained our business. Perfect, fabulous cloud like scones cooked in a slow combustion wood stove. As high as high could be, smothered in delicious homemade strawberry jam and fresh yummy cream, they were to die for!

It came without trouble and with many compliments, including a group of Americans who walked through my door one lonely Monday morning when there was no sun about.

Can you imagine what it was like suddenly hearing the most profound singing that lifted the heavy air and brought the sunshine in? The group that just 'dropped in' turned out to be the most respected Christian choir in America.

They asked me what was my favorites tune. My mind went blank, but then they broke out and sang with gusto 'Amazing Grace'. I broke down.

"How did you know that was my special song of all?"

Utah's Reverend Martin Phillips and his world-travelling troupe called in again over the next couple of years, and in his letter (which I still have), thanked me again for what he said was the 'best Devonshire tea in Australia'. I only ever needed that skill whilst living at Riverwood House.

When looking back now, Riverwood House Bed and Breakfast/Restaurant was a timely escape, a distraction from our emotional issues of life's dealings.

Clearly recognizing God's stated purpose for me was to, "give comfort to those in need," exposed during the time of my son's troubles, I was tested over and again, and by unusual circumstances.

For example, folk appearing out of the blue, looking after them and realising later... well... that was interesting? For instance, a dear friend called in to Riverwood, stating he really wanted to see me before he passed away with colon cancer. It was a beautiful goodbye. Over the next few days, his grieving family welcomed the precious prayers for his rest.

Again, a young woman arrived at 6am with her two little children. They had camped outside all night unbeknown to me. Tired, fragile and very hungry, they received a good breakfast and freshly baked muffins with an agreement for later payment before they headed off for another destination.

In the late afternoon of that day my incoming guests from Denmark, near Albany, informed me that she was a run-away and the police were looking for her and the children. She had left her car full of clothing and children's belongings in our back shed. She did return, though not happy that her things were at the police station for safe-keeping.

The Blues Festival was the following week where enthusiastic crowds were expected to eat and enjoy music in the grounds of Riverwood House.

Another occasion was when an unaccompanied, well-dressed young lad ended up on the doorstep expecting to go to a job he thought existed. Sensing his mental affliction, I allowed this likeable lad of gentle manners to help me with that constant hard chore of cutting wood in return for keep until his mother drove the 300 kilometres to return him to his Perth home.

There are numerous accounts of being led. One was an actual warning sign to save a young life during a fellowship meeting. A few days after this event, I was shattered to realise what it was that was being said in tongues. The beautiful, gifted young man had been killed right outside his parents' property.

Another profound moment was when three Irish friends gathered at Riverwood House for a Devonshire tea. When the host woman mentioned a problem with her back, my hand reached out and touched her gently. The reaction was immediate from her two friends exclaiming they also felt the sheer force of the energy that flowed through to reach them at the other side of the shared table. This happens often in one form or another.

"As I am part of you, you are part of me."

Riverwood House to me was a beautiful experience of peaceful river walks, geese, roosters, love-birds, ferret, quinces, fresh veggies from the opposite markets, young babes, beautiful food, enthusiastic patrons, winter sunshine and most of all, the making of precious life-long friends.

It proved to be a rewarding adventure for me, meeting folk from all over the world and clairvoyants who confirmed the existence of the doctor's ghost in what was his clinic room.

Riverwood House was also a mixed experience, both trying and uplifting. I truly loved the stunning historic home that sat beside the bridge in Bridgetown, the pretty South West Australian country town. I clearly remember the feelings of absolute gratitude to experience the music emanating from the 200 birds gathered on the front entry lawn and meetings where one could not hear because of the bird song and chatter. How we loved the friendly country folk and riverside markets.

The wheel of life churns slowly to clear away the stones. The stones became heavy with emotional upheaval. My dream of building a lovely retirement home on our land in Walter Road, Bridgetown was gone. Bridgetown had reached saturation point in the competition for both accommodation and dining experiences, it took its toll. The dramatic downturn in real estate sales resulted in Riverwood House taking many months to sell.

Incredibly, Christopher, the toddler son of the next owners, was a splitting image of the Riverwood's first owner's only son. As Bridgetown's first doctor this valued man was killed within metres of his beautiful riverside home.

Meanwhile, my guests questioned what my next adventure would be. Well, that was easy! The long-awaited Reflexology and to travel around Australia, the amazing country I call my own.

HEALTH AND STUDY

Reflexology and travel were long-held dreams, in fact, ever since my son was ten years old and suffering so much with chronic bronchitis.

At that time, I had picked up 'The Stories that Feet Can Tell', by Eunice Ingham. I was intrigued by the thought that mere pressure on a reflex point on the upper pad of the hand could relieve Bronchitis. The mustard seed arrived.

Emotional and financial restraints came before

achievement. It proved to be a challenging time choosing a new home, overcoming accidents, illness and discontent.

Through the challenge of studying this healing art at the age of fifty-five years of age, I found even more connection with the friendship needed at that time offered by the Sheltering Tree Pentecostal community. Ironically, their logo was the mustard tree.

From there came the experience of the born-again commitment, yet because of fear experienced by some, I felt totally alone with no caring or interested family to witness. This was very difficult to take, even though my faith has been with me since childhood, faced as part of the journey I knew I had to take.

Investigations into my continual tiredness proved copper poisoning had a good hold on my body. My fellow naturopathy students told me some time later that they knew how sick I was. Yet I managed to get through my studies and become a qualified Reflexologist.

One colleague from that study time, Patricia Bell, remains a valued peer today. I am grateful for the journey into the ancient art and where it led me.

The magical experiences kept on coming and the knowing kept on growing. When I look back I say to myself gosh, that was amazing!

THE GREATNESS OF THE KNOWING

In 2003, my husband supported my decision to try our hand at selling coffee via the local markets, with one day being spent with the supplier learning the ropes.

Returning home via an uneventful deviation to see my oldest friend Nancy, the opportunity came to call in and see my son at his hospital workplace. He appeared thrilled to see me and introduced me to a woman he appreciated, whose sleeping 92-year-old mother was a patient nearing the end of her time.

With her daughter's permission, the guiding hand again took me, to have me on my knees by her side quietly praying, ending with the words, "peace, peace, peace."

Amazingly, she opened her eyes with clarity and repeated, "peace, peace, peace."

Her daughter and I held each other tightly as a most brilliant embracing golden glow surrounded us, and I felt her crumple further into my arms. Oh! My Lord, thank you so much.

The dear old frail woman passed away shortly after but not before her grand-daughter approached me when I was ready to leave, though I may not have been able to help her crumbling marriage.

On the 24 May 2004, I was abruptly awoken by a

thundering voice in my head, "hail God."

I quickly scribbled with sleepy eyes my understanding, and 'Hallgarten' is what I wrote.

The next day I searched for the meaning through the internet and what emerged was an image of Mary and the Christ Child set on a yellow shield, from an area I found to be Brussels.

This pleased me immensely as I have always felt that somewhere along the way another life involved convents and prayer, even though I am not of the Catholic faith. What also came through was Hildegard von Bingen. She was born in 1106 in West Franconia (now Germany) and is considered one of the first female liberationists of her time. She wrote the most exquisite poetry and music, and was a brilliant medic and herbalist. It wasn't the first encounter.

Before leaving that Sheltering Tree community a vision that appeared as clear as the finest day stated, "Look to the hill on the left and this will be your home."

When my husband and I took off on our long-service adventure in July 2004 and arrived at the Cygnet Bay Pearl Farm, the three-bedroom house that was ours for three months at no cost was right opposite the office block, the hill was to the left.

We both had a wonderful time whilst there and I passed the 40 days and 40 nights in safety after my born-again experience. Again, what I felt was acknowledgement of an arrow piercing my back that I recognized as Hildegard.

It was a time of peace, of further study and enjoyment. Olympic Games, scintillating Sunday walks on the beachfront at One Arm Point collecting old trochus shells, the extra-ordinary Cape Leveque, whale watching from a boating afternoon to Sunday Island and the brilliant warmth of the sun. Exploring the bush to find amazing Bower birds (that pinched blue earrings if one wasn't careful), brilliant flowers and the fascination of watching the sea re-claim the mangroves within moments after being half a kilometre away.

I was over-the-moon to find the stunning Kalbarri stone that lined my floors at home. The sheer beauty of these amazing, ancient pink stones, captured in treasured photographs. Sapphire crabs by the millions on the beach and finding many sting-rays' sleeping holes. The three-month long service leave disappeared so quickly.

The dongas that I used to attend to at the Cygnet Bay Pearl Farm have since been transformed into comfortable lodgings for the many paying visitors that now see their way to this gorgeous place.

STUDY TO PRACTITIONER

In 2005, the dream of becoming a practicing Reflexologist came to fruition and was given an extra boost.

With the continuing guiding hand leading the way, I secured valuable work within the Armadale Home Help Service, and a New Enterprise Incentive Scheme $10,000 grant (without interview). I was earning a good income and assistance all the way from management. It is interesting to note that Bedfordale Hill is also to the left of my home at Mt Richon (sold in June 2015).

Due to continuing unhealthy influences and lack of emotional support, my body decided to take its own course of action by revealing a serious sciatica problem that had me bedridden for months.

Following this, in January 2006 I experienced a very nasty fall from a high ladder. I landed on brick paving, with my head impacting on a sharp border stone in the garden. My family acted quickly, with the ambulance arriving within five minutes, followed by eight hours of unconsciousness. Life doing my head in?

Animosity also raged between father and son about my care, and my lack of adequate response due to a bruised brain.

AWAY AT LAST

It took perseverance in recovering from the head injury to win my heavy vehicle L licence. I needed it so that my husband and I could finally get away in our treasured, long yearned for Winnebago, a bronze beauty of which we were so proud.

Saying goodbye to my dad, Max, at his nursing home on the morning of the around Australia departure, he and I both knew that it was last hug ever. We both fought back the tears.

I felt lost while packing up the beautiful home of four years. It was a struggle so soon after the accident, even with paid help.

Remembering the slightest thing was difficult during the initial stages of our trip around the Top End. However, this was part of my destiny, it gave the time to seek out the places and the people who were to colour my life even more.

Over the next few weeks of travel within our home state of Western Australia, several fellow travellers became firm friends and later enjoyed our hospitality during our time in Darwin and in the Daintree.

My faith helped all the way, for my memory continued to suffer for at least eighteen months, adding to the depression, stress and misunderstandings.

We drove through flooding rains that March and April to reach and spend three weeks working on a cattle station on the edge of the Gibson Desert. This gave us insight to this beautiful, yet incredibly harsh land, fat cattle, camels, horses and green Spinifex.

Spirit again moved through my husband. He found a book in the station kitchen area, 'Anatomy of the Spirit–The Seven Stages of Power and Healing' by the renowned medical interpretive author, Caroline Myss.

Her book revealed the Seven Sacred Chakras and their relevance. This book gave many hours of pleasure and study for me to understand more about energy and its ancient connections. I find that many things from Spirit have come via my husband, bless him, who still has difficulty understanding my ways and my mission.

During a relaxing six weeks in cosmopolitan Broome awaiting parts for our Winnebago, sadly my sister rang to tell me that our Dad, Max, had passed away. It seemed hardly any time at all after our departure.

However, even though he was extremely ill, he achieved what he wanted in his own home not lived in for some time, his beer and his brawn sandwich and his wife and kids. All too soon his heart began to fail before they could be totally enjoyed. Dear Dad, I loved you heaps.

I returned home to celebrate my Dad's life and a

beautiful funeral, and to spend a few days with my mother before returning to Broome.

Moving further north brought lazy days around dams along the highways, new and frightening experiences in dealing with my husband's sudden serious illness in Derby, his recovery and the blessed company with cherished family. Then to Kununurra! Such a beautiful place.

What remains so strong in my mind are the times when I was completely alone, along the recently flooded Fitzroy River and later climbing the hill to view the dry red chasm of the Ord River dam overflow.

Alone to give thanks for the beauty and to feel and receive intense energy that streamed into my outspread hands, tingling and warming me all over and again giving thanks for that gift. That is something no man can take from me.

The very next day a group of Canning Stock route piggy back adventurers queued to have foot Reflexology to relieve their aches and pains from so much rough travel.

I swam alone in the cool waters and revelled at the privilege of swimming in the massive man-made icon that is the lifeblood of Kununurra.

The Golden Orb spiders' astonishing network of webs that caught the light and looked like pure gold, the strongest of the all spider webs of nature that left one feeling rather humble. Charlie Sharp, the owner of the Lake Argyle Resort and born in this area, assured me of the intense spirituality that flows through this area. I truly believed him.

INTO THE NORTHERN TERRITORY

Another message kept coming to mind whilst enjoying the truly magical beauty of the Douglas-Daly area in the Northern Territory.

My husband and I had the most peaceful and enjoyable time living in our Winnebago right on the banks of this river, watching the birds do their dance at dusk over the glassy waters.

A thought came again and again on our approach to Darwin. "Jan Hordern, Jan Hordern!"

I cut out the advertisement and kept it safe intending to treat my head injury with Reflexology.

Without effort we managed to secure tenure at the Darwin Basketball Stadium grounds in exchange for opening and closing the largest basketball courts in Australia. It was the beginning of a nine-month adventure.

It was an invigorating time being involved with the rush of two thousand young and old in the biggest basketball centre in Australia. The evenings were sublime, the work mundane and the experience worthwhile. Everyone loved our dog Guiness and he, as always, was a great comfort.

Graham, a befriended fellow traveller living next to us in the sporting precinct in Darwin, arranged for me to meet his Reiki master friend, Lorraine. It was my first experience with this gentle and caressing treatment.

She kept mentioning that her own neck felt strange. My injury was reflecting in her own body. Lorraine later drew my attention to what she felt as an incredible power held within me, that my energy was so strong and stressed acknowledgment. The traveller card I picked was listening. Had I been listening to what my body was telling me?

I took the plunge and enrolled with Reiki Master, Jan Hordern, who further encouraged me to discover more about who I am. She also predicted that I would teach Reflexology.

Concentrated meditation and fine attunements required for passing the First Ursui Reiki degree brought forth an explosion of memories, languages and incidents. Jan's vision felt right, that coincided and gave reason to why I would suddenly speak extra languages.

On the second attunement, my vision clearly reflected being a finely dressed American Indian squaw carrying a badly injured shoulder with my husband dying in my arms.

This event totally turned my world upside down. I felt as if I had been in a tornado, the earth spinning as I sat down to recover in her beautiful garden.

This also reinforced a vision I had in 2003 where oriental writings flashed through my mind. What looked like a pile of scribble after awakening, now embedded in my mind. To this day, I use this art intuitively and honour the gift accordingly.

During the final session, my fellow Reiki students had gathered around a Chinese colleague awaiting her turn on the treatment table. As I held my hands over her crown chakra, another profound experience occurred. My vision was of a young Chinese girl who appeared before a magnificent mountainous valley, to the left was a cave.

Her fringed hair was covered with an exquisite bonnet of black silk embossed with colourful embroidery. The name 'Poo Chin' came forth.

I take this opportunity to thank Jan and the delightful fellowship with our Reiki colleagues, and her comforting front patio and yummy snacks!

The group was enthralled at just how well crystals enhance one's own energy field in the exercises we did.

What followed was a divergence into crystals, rushes of healing sensations tearing through my body at all hours of the night, and the ability to dream-walk. It was at Jan's home that a new name emerged, 'Amethyst Star Child'. The recently acquired valuable moldavite crystal had its effect.

Some six months into the caretaking/work duties at the stadium, the atmosphere changed. Animosity existed between the management and one staff member we had developed a good friendship with. The karma was undeniably off and I yearned to move on.

However, I was encouraged to wait, because Darwin was preparing for their bi-yearly Arafura Games. That year was a special one, with the Para-Olympics trials basketball competitions with international teams, including the United States of America, Japan and Korea. It was worth staying.

There were some funny moments when our gorgeous Guiness decided he really liked to investigate all the free-standing shoed legs lying about. Those matches were the gutsiest ever witnessed. Men of steel in wheelchairs, just brilliant and far more interesting than the Wildcat Basketball team performances. It was also gratifying to watch the numerous gatherings in this sporting bastion of graduating police cadets proudly being acknowledged by the VIPs of Darwin.

Prior to our leaving our tenure at the Darwin Basketball Stadium in 2007, one of my jobs was to sell tickets for the basketball games. When ticket sales slowed, I ventured onto a website and discovered a dream job, that of property manager for a unique Daintree home.

It brought back teenage memories of seeing on a black and white television screen the ancient forest that was then truly wild. I became excited and applied. Success there was not. Linda, the owner, gave me an assurance she would keep our details on file and that consequently fuelled more passion to get to this sacred place.

We also made some timely friends with whom we shared experiences. A newly found friend, Rosemary, encouraged me to stay on for a while longer in Darwin. She and Dennis gave us a great gift by offering to me at a Reiki afternoon to look after our shitzu, Guiness, whilst we explored Kakadu, something we will never forget.

We then had the privilege of looking after her and Dennis' lovely home in Moil and their treasured pet whilst they went to Melbourne for the same amount of time.

It was there that more profound experiences developed. Some incidences would be what others may think as unbelievable, some confirmed by people we knew, especially Robyn who worked with us at the basketball centre.

Rosemary and Dennis Scrutton's home was full of natural therapy books that had assisted Rosemary's recovery from cancer. I was in clover!

Their beautiful, fruitful garden set the scene for Reflexology for a young very pregnant mum worried that she had not felt movement for quite a few days. What a special occasion that was, working the feet and feeling the grateful outcome of stirring life. We trust she and her babe are doing well.

One evening on the veranda, I had been quietly reading Louise Hay's book on Angels. Upon retiring and going to the bathroom there in the mirror was a face I had not seen before, myself, appearing twenty years younger with a bright, balanced look in the eye. It was just like the photo I had taken at my son's fabulous wedding in 2000 where I was at a completely happy place with life. I remember glowing at my son's actions of lifting his beautiful, injured Sinead above his waist, holding her up high in his arms when he danced the wedding waltz.

The Kakadu experiences were quite profound. The sacred sites stirred old memories and made me feel so grateful to be part of this diverse, colourful and amazing country called Australia. The Northern Territory had made its mark!

FAR NORTH QUEENSLAND

We made an easy journey down to Three Ways, in the middle of the Northern Territory, then across the great plains of North Queensland to Richmond.

A work opportunity for my husband in what was advertised as a winery was an eye-opener. The unusual winery was owned by a business man who manipulated various wines and fruit juices with retailed wines to produce some stunning award-winning products. I felt initially that this may not have been a good move and eventually my feelings proved true.

Ingham is an interesting town, heavily influenced by Italian culture. Seeing sugar cane trains operating through the centre of town was amusing to us.

I did seriously look at further study towards accredited certification, but somehow, something was not quite right. However, I am ever so grateful for meeting a group of women therapists who were partaking in a weekend workshop at the stunning heritage property.

They were all from Townsville. They introduced me to the Emotional Freedom Technique being taught that weekend while I provided them with reflexology. It was a new learning curve in discovering proven new ideas in the quest to help my fellow man.

I downloaded the eighty-page manual during the

two-week time out housesitting in Cairns. It was a time when I further developed the new interest of EFT, where one can assist oneself healing by tapping on external meridian points to clear away issues that damaged the energy body.

Cairns proved to be a discovery adventure! I loved exploring alone splendid gorges, breathtaking scenery, finding magnificent Ulysses butterflies floating above the air of Crystal Brook and the extensive Kuranda markets where I found the trilogy of The Celestine Prophecy. That sparked that extra interest in encouraging all to reach a higher potential and for a better existence. That book also spoke strongly to my Spirit.

Moving northwards towards Julatten in September 2007 our next stop was the sacred World War II site of Tolga (just out of Atherton Tablelands). I awoke one morning visualising the most brilliant pastel colours, from a sleep that was so profoundly refreshing. My mother later told me she heard me tapping at her window at her home in Perth.

"It was your voice Marylin." My mother still talks about my dream walk to this day.

Julatten caravan park proved to be an extremely beautiful spot where we again connected to precious family and dear friends in the area at the same time. Cape House never left my mind, even to the point where I rang Linda and asked to lay brochures there, even though it was over an hour away from Julatten. That was in the October.

The assignment at the Julatten caravan park was totally weird, and I got to see how other people lived and hid from society.

CAPE HOUSE OF THE DAINTREE

I began to yearn for home. Christmas time was always a challenge for me as I missed family, my mother, and all the grandchildren. The youngest, Sian, was only two years old. I returned home for three weeks and enjoyed every moment.

During my escape from confined living I accepted a Queensland phone call at my daughter's Bunbury home on my birthday. It was Linda, the Cape House owner, "Marylin, would you like to come and have a cup of coffee with me and discuss the opportunity of looking after Cape House for us?"

What a birthday present! Never give up your dreams. During a four-hour interview and property tour with the owners my husband graciously accepted, deciding on the spot that this is what we would do. For the next twelve months, we lived the dream.

On 145 acres of virgin ancient forest, including 15 acres of mature orchard, Cape House is an amazing Thai-style home of 300 square metres, built with soaring timbers from the old Cairns brewery. Its front balconies were high in the air and the view overlooked the Daintree River and across to Port Douglas.

One could bathe amongst the trees, if one doesn't mind the odd snake or two venturing in, or the tiny fruit bats that flew catching the fire flies in the evening light. How I loved that home.

I am so proud of my husband and the way he handled the many issues living off the land presented. Solar, wind and water power, all to be monitored and cared for in all types of weather.

I can laugh now of the time when he suggested we push a wheelbarrow down to the broken water supply motor that one had to pass through Lawyer vine and waterfalls to get to. The motor weighed 60 kilos!

Now imagine if you can, climbing two metres up a slippery, muddy, high slope with just vines and minimal rope to hang on to, disconnect the motor, lowering it to water level, load it up onto the wheelbarrow and backtrack to the vehicle over the waterfall and stony creek. It took at least an hour to get back to the roadway. Then days later, repeating it all to re-install the repaired motor.

The Daintree remains one of the most special places and time of my life, both happy and sad, and I can safely say that of my husband. We found it a privilege to be there, even though it was hard work for us at times and coping with the humidity, slippery mud, mold and mosquitoes during the wet season was trying.

I came through several not so nice experiences such as scrub-typhus, Giardia, and urticaria from paper-wasp attacks. Then there was a freak accident, again injuring my shoulders. A definite struggle for my immune system that was compromised so many years before.

Looking back, I feel it is no coincidence that in this life my shoulders suffered so much. My Mossman doctor exclaimed, "This is an incredibly old injury!"

She indicated an impact had split the joint right down the middle (perhaps from a fall earlier in my life or past life?). Injuries continued to occur.

The jungle appeared to speak to me, to envelope me in its timelessness and beauty. We rejoiced when others shared that experience with us. I also hold the jungle responsible for my aura changing from deep burgundy red to the most brilliant indigo blue, emerald green and white. What more could one ask for? Spiritual growth confirmed!

A friend, a professional photographer, took a brilliant photo of what the Daintree means to me, a jungle bird feeding from an exquisite flowered tree in the immediate vicinity of Cape House yard.

Cape House provided many wonders. Oh, to watch

the storms come in with clouds at varying levels and between levels of mountains in the distance. The Daintree River ebbing and flowing four times a day, Port Douglas and the Coral Sea and the feeling of living in the tree tops with flocks of birds soaring in the air currents. The strength found to tackle projects because of the isolation, of battling with the Lawyer vine that grasps one like a vengeance.

Enjoyment found in everyday companionship like mowing the fifteen acres in tandem, and as my husband has always said, watching the lawn grow overnight. Observing the flooding rains that disappear, in most cases, as quickly as they had appeared.

We enjoyed such precious times spent with family and friends, and what we felt to be valued friends of the owners when they managed some much sought-after rest and recreation from their Sydney lifestyle. We experienced happy guests and sensational weddings.

Such was the life. With that happiness, also sadness showed its face once again. Our treasured Guiness became extremely ill after we had ventured to Yungaburra for me to teach Reflexology to some nurses who worked in the Cairns Hospital region.

Now I feel regret at having to scold him because he would not walk, he just refused to budge. Little did we know that his heart was failing. After spending a night at the veterinary clinic, my precious Guiness died in my arms on the way back to Cape House. I will never forget his frightened, gasping face struggling for his final breath.

Hugh and I both sobbed and sobbed at the roadside. Wrapped in his woolen rug, his little body remained warm for hours. It was with a heavy, breaking heart that I buried him deeply near a recently planted lychee tree.

We managed to find a remnant piece of marble to place on top in the endeavour to keep him whole in his final sleep. Two days later whilst sitting inside this stunning house I turned to see his ghost flash by. He never leaves me. His Spirit is so strong with me that he has appeared in my dreams, represented by a shining whiteness integrated with my Soul. Thank you!

Before leaving the magical place, I heard the forest beg me to stay, "don't go... don't go..."

I was torn, homesick for family, and my son's wife Sinead had just given birth to the final grandchild. I was missing seeing my four other grandchildren as well.

Confirmation came through by an offer for a position as caretakers for the Yarloop Steam Workshops. Yet I was torn about whether to stay and finish our adventure.

That Christmas we invited our only grandson, Jacob, to return with me from my Christmas break in Perth and experience the Daintree before travelling in our Winnebago with us back to Perth.

He loved it, bat poo and all. He was a delight and mixed well with Linda's daughter Ruby who was the same age. We discovered what an engaging young man he is, with a mind that never ceased to amaze me.

YARLOOP

Working with my cousin Ron behind the counter of the historical Yarloop Steam Workshops Post Office was an interesting time.

I loved the contact with his customers and found the curator at that time, Geoff Fortune, his wife Val and their friend Dawn understanding companions. They provided many a laugh.

One such Post Office customer was heavily involved with Riding for the Disabled at Fairbridge Village. We connected instantly, like attracts like. Anne is a Reiki master. It saddens me greatly that this historical place was destroyed by fire in February 2016, just a few months before completing my story. Geoff Fortune's knowledge is irreplaceable, and I am so glad this very elderly gentleman spent his senior life telling the story of Yarloop.

DARK CLOUDS

Destructive influences again showed through the cracks because of unsatisfactory living and work capacity, and issues encountered with the then tenants in our beautiful Perth suburban home.

During a regular maintenance inspection of the Mt Richon home my instincts kicked in big time. My reasoning and the standing hairs on the back of my neck indicated the necessity to write down the licence number of this second vehicle in the driveway.

One hour on my husband and I discovered the drug set up in the outside workshop, and all the paraphernalia required to produce illicit drugs. After a very tense wait, the Drug Squad raided our house and arrested the two parties.

It is a time I would rather forget, yet know it is important to remember. It also had the effect of hardening one's attitude in business, sometimes in the negative sense. Further tenants who appeared at first to be genuine took the advantage. Although one prefers to trust, life presents challenges not to one's liking. However, under every dark cloud there is a silver lining. The Spirit was not yet finished.

FAIRBRIDGE VILLAGE

Fairbridge Village was familiar to me, as I had previously volunteered for Kalparrin in 2005, providing Reflexology for the mothers of very sick children.

This event in 2009 left its mark. So did Fairbridge. I leant over the banister rails and stated loudly to my colleagues, "I'd really like to live here."

Following up on that instinct an inquiry to reception area revealed a negative status. Two months later, with Spirit working through Anne from Yarloop, the care-taking position that offered some financial freedom was in hand, being at the right place and the right time with no formal interview. Thank you again Spirit.

After nearly four years living at Fairbridge, one appreciates the beauty of nature, the trees, the clear stars at night and involvement with this charitable organisation.

Great times with very dear family members were treasured and the grandchildren left to swim and roam its beautiful acres. Fun times and fabulous music at the independent Fairbridge Festival brings thousands to be as one big family, all camped on every nook and cranny of grass available. In early spring, an inundation of magnificent horses and their caring owners enjoy a cross-country event that encompasses the rolling green hillsides.

CHINA AND THE GROWING KNOWING

The knowing was evident when I received an invitation via The Australian Reflexology Association in 2010 to take part in a study trip to China in April 2011. Having that card in my hand felt right and stirred deep emotions.

This time and place at Fairbridge was emotionally a difficult one for me, as my Spirit felt ready to fly and achieve wonderful things. There were times when my morale was so low.

One instance a request came before I left for China from Nancy, the woman I considered my second mum, to help her change her financial arrangements as she felt there was something not quite right.

The consequences of this were devastating at the time. Positives came forth in the flow of writings that had only been spasmodic over previous years, culminating in a collection of over forty-five soul writings, 'I AM the Messenger – Messages of Love to Stir the Soul.'

Before embarking on this remarkable journey to a land that called to me, my concern was for my heart-loved sister-in-law experiencing ill health. I asked my husband how he would cope with her leaving us, as they were true soul mates. He didn't comprehend my meaning.

China was amazing. As a small group of five we were

treated with dignity and servility. I learned a great deal and felt as one, fascinated with this ancient culture and its peoples. It was an incredible trip, visiting The World Health Organisation lectures at the 80,000-strong student Shanghai Traditional Chinese Medicine University in cherry blossom time.

We toured hospital establishments with their directors and attended a full day practical lecture/workshop. I cannot express enough the grandeur of the Shanghai University museum and the impact it had on me. So, incredible to view items many thousands of years old related to my chosen practice.

Our very first eye-opening experience of overnight Chinese first class train travel was to Tai'an, and the shared joy of coming across Australians studying at the universities.

Top Tai'an hospital staff dedicated the following full day to our small group, followed by interaction with their students in massage, acupuncture and reflexology. The intoxicating bitter herbs bubbling away on old tiled benches and gas flames, and then getting packaged in automatic machines made me smile. One does not forget the aroma, what I considered was primitive to our standards.

However, the pharmacy was extraordinary. Magnificent wooden structures with hundreds of herbs neatly packaged ready for the hospital to send out to their patients. Patients were holistically treated with their traditional ways, for example remaining in care for a fortnight for acupuncture.

An exhilarating experience to visit the ancient Tao Temple on the top of Mount Tai. Its 6000 steps and many hundreds of thousands of locals enjoying their special time there threw us in the deep end. I say with confidence that our group really enjoyed Tai'an, and especially its peoples' markets in both food and commerce.

The awesome and humbling work and respect of the Chinese people in restoring the Terracotta Warriors and to traverse the walls of the ancient city of Xian lives in my mind forever.

We saw the Shen Shun monk warriors achieving incredible feats. Joyfully, on one of the last nights in Beijing, I danced the women's fan dance with total strangers. Our group explored some of the Forbidden City and mingled with women from thousands of miles away having the same experience. Amazing Beijing.

Best of all was the exertion of the climb to ring the huge brass warning bell on the longest wall on earth. This was very satisfying.

When my Chinese vision from Darwin was mentioned to my Chinese guide Jing on the 2nd day of that study trip in to China, he stared at me intently and strongly verbalized, "No! Not Poo Chin. You have seen Quan Yin, her temple is in Repulse Bay, Shanghai."

Jing and I were both saddened to think that Shanghai was the previous day's stopover. I am reminded of another time of an arrow shot through me when watching a program of Sapa in Far North Vietnam. There on that television screen were the women in their brightly embroidered bonnets. Sapa, Queen of the Mountain, overlooked by towering mountains and within an incredible valley, my vision from the Darwin reiki workshop.

Considering my strange questions to my husband before I left on this trip, it is no surprise to me that during the last week in China I plainly experienced unsettling feelings that I now recognise as the start of mourning for someone precious, and commented on by my travel colleague. The phone communications from my husband concerning his sister Beryl began to flow during that last week in China.

Guidance and assistance came at every step on the return journey from that far away land. The aircraft arrived on time, then the Customs officer selected me early with no problems with my declarations. A different exit was chosen where a vacant taxi was available for a quick getaway to my mother's home, where my husband was waiting. Then down to Fairbridge to prepare for the five-hour journey to Albany.

It was truly a blessing that both of us spoke to the very last gasping phone call Beryl made.

"I am dying. I just want to thank you for being my friend."

With that I replied, "Yes Beryl, thank you too, it's time for you to go."

This still brings me to tears in remembrance of our feelings towards each other. Thankfully, we arrived in Albany safely from a worrying night trip, free from kangaroo danger on the road, knowing that time was of the essence. With only minutes to spare my husband held his soul mate one last time before she lapsed into unconsciousness.

Yet the morning of her passing, the home she shared with Allan felt full of her presence. Prior to writing a eulogy my goodbye was an emotional one and her Spirit attracted my attention with the flash of the room lights. It was a bright and beautiful day. So pleased to think her spirit was there, for her loved children Martin, Fiona, Allan and family.

THE PASSING OVERS

Dealing with imminent death is no stranger. My instincts relentlessly drove me on many occasions to be there for the last moments.

Apart from the Bridgetown endeavours, a friend's passing took me by surprise. Whilst showering one morning, fierce sensations doubled up my body, yet no pain, and I groaned repeatedly.

There appeared to be no explanation at that time for the cause of this much anxiety. Two weeks later my husband's next door neighbour spoke to me early in the afternoon to say that our close friend's wife had passed on.

She had died from a heart attack in her sleep that early morning, and was found by a very distraught family at noon when trying to wake her. This was the time to give comfort and consolation to my friend Ernie, after praying for his wife's soul to make a safe transition to her next journey.

One other occasion that reminds me that sometimes words pop out of the mouth without prior thought (against thoughtlessness), happened after the funeral service of my mother's dear sister. The family were congregating with refreshments in hand. I knew that my cousin was experiencing difficulties with a terminal illness from an innocent event.

"I would like to see you when the time comes." The words came out, to the astonished look on both he and his wife's face.

One very uncomfortable day in summer, sometime later, Perth experienced the worst dew point ever. The news came that Ron was poorly. Again, the knowing kicked in and demanded my presence at his bedside, much to the confusion in my family.

However, it was a distraction from the awful weather. This event is always remembered with humility because of Ron's gracious manner in accepting the outcome.

His feet looked like that of a newborn, not a mark, soft yet white, indicating what was to come. Gentle feet, for a gentle soul. Ron passed on the next morning. He was my Uncle Jack's only son.

The following years saw another two friends further their journey. My oldest friend since I was born, Nancy, lost her son to diabetes. He lacked the courage to face the world any longer with his blindness and took the long road with an epileptic fit that left him unconscious for three weeks.

It was on a winter's day in July when the life support switched off. Such a difficult decision for although his heart beat strongly his mind did not.

I kept hoping for a response that would allow the intelligent, wonderfully musical man who was only two months older than I, to again aspire to life. Not to be!

Together, his mother, my mother and the understanding nurse stood holding hands whilst I prayed gently in tongues for his safe passage through the Heavenly Gate. His beautiful music collection was part of his legacy.

Neighbours can be such a delight, and so was Geoff, a super intelligent and friendly soul. His battle with the creeping cancer was eventually lost at Hollywood Hospital. The knowing had called me once again, when I happened to be nearby at the time. He was so thrilled to see me in his very distressed state of mind, "I am so glad to see you... I've been asking for you."

The head Palliative Care Chinese doctor commented, "How fortunate to have reflexology Geoff, wish it was me having a treatment."

Calmed and sleeping before I left for home, I later discovered he journeyed on the next morning. He is one friend missed every time I look to the home next door. Thank you for being in my life.

The knowing grew stronger. Spirit helped me once again through contact with a profoundly gifted woman who taught me to trust my Spirit again, the I AM that lives within me. She firmly stated knowing of my past lives and what I am now. Her aid in also providing guidance during a time of extreme anxiety was welcoming and calming.

PEN TO PAPER

These past several years have been a turning point of being told to get it to print, to downsize by moving away from dear friends. Moving to a place that has the freshest sea breezes and suburban beauty. Time to establish friendships with like-minded individuals who share my philosophy in life.

It has been a time to tabulate the many exquisite automatic writings that have guided me over the past twenty-two years or so. They contain encouragement for me to continue at times when I felt life was a hard slog.

Over the next months to years, the outpourings of emotions were finally put to paper, any time of the day and night, with the occasional break.

These writings contain messages that sometimes affect us all. They still bring tears to my eyes and absolute peace when picked up in time of need.

Workshops witnessed what we can achieve as God Spirits in the human body. Our choice is to love and provide compassion to our fellow man, to observe and to continue learning about ourselves and what can be achieved with belief in

Ehyeh Asher Ehyeh
I Am That I Am.

My following writings were relevant to an exploratory period of renewing faith, study at the age of fifty-five years into natural complementary health and challenging family situations.

DEW DROPS AND GLITTER

Dew drops and glitter after the rain
Reach to my heart and help ease the pain
Of wondering... yet knowing...
Of what life will bring
Bringing me closer to Jesus my King.

Dew drops and glitter
And birds are a flutter
Dashing and darting amongst all the cover
Of sparkling dew drops
And sunbeams and other
Of God's wondrous things.

To start the day with a smile of my face
And joy in my heart
I thank you my Grace.

MY TREES

Green on brown cream on brown
Outwardly stretching waiting to be seen
The beauty is outstanding
Reaching deep into my heart
To store for the days when there is no sun about.

Outwardly stretching
With birds on their limbs
Darting and singing without a whim
How gorgeous they are
Their songs fill the senses
Magpies and sunshine and trees and their limbs.

Gliding along from tree to roost
Inquisitive stare and looks that could say
Well, where is my meal... I'm singing away
Beautiful magpies four times a day.

And kookaburras too, now that's a great one
Such a delight to have them feed from
Your hand each night
And touch their feathers ever so soft
What God has given me...
Oh! Such a lot.

And Guiness beside me loyal and true
Soft and pale tail with a gentle hue
His funny face and ungainly gait
And for that back scratch he just can't wait.

Yes, my Guiness is kind
and my Guiness is good
Curled up inside his little domain
Snoring and dreaming of a chase in the wood.

The three years from 2002 to 2005 were complicated with lots happening both in business, spiritually and with family. It was a time of vivid dreams and delving into their meaning.

I often had the knowing that at some level in a past life the church or even a convent was at the forefront. This also is reinforced with hearing 'Hail God Hildegarde' in one dream.

Abbess Hilda von Bingen lived in the millennium 1000, producing music that is still aired today. She was a fine herbalist who had the ear of the Pope at that time, a very rare occurrence in those days.

I have often felt her presence, especially during the extra-ordinary three months of 2004 spent living and working on the Cygnet Bay Pearl Farm. During this unusual time, furthering my knowledge of natural therapies and loving life in the warmth of the tropical sun, the following powerful message was received.

TAKE THY BROTHER'S HAND

Take thy brother's hand
No matter whence he came
His color should not matter
Nor his thinking be to blame.

Take thy brother's hand
And give him Love abound
Help him overcome
Those burdens so often found.

Take thy brother's hand
And share the joy with him
Of knowing Christ Our Saviour
And the Light that lives within.

Focusing on the above expression, does it reflect what is happening in this world today, in Europe, Africa and war tragedies? Families losing their homes, traveling thousands of kilometers with only what is on their backs and the responsibility borne on many nations for their safety.

It would be some time before the magic appeared again, mainly because of trauma from a horrendous high fall and my memory taking time to recover. However, on Easter Friday night in Darwin, 2007, the following words began to flow, and to this day have more relevance than ever.

THE ASCENSION POEM

When the stars align with planets
And the Lord is on his way
You will pick up the cross
And use it to clear the way.

Our Lord has been waiting
For this precious hour
Descending into Glory
And full ultimate power.

Our Lord has not diminished
In his shining power
He has grown to meet the Son's full strength.

Is this the final hour?

Some years after receiving the above piece, a Reflexology client questioned, "Do you know who your guide is?"

I knew there were three, including a very old man.

"No," she said, "he is not your father. He is very ancient, and I think from the Shetland Islands. He is carrying an upside down cross."

This work still has a very unsettling effect on me. I have questioned the above meanings many times over the years.

We know that recently the stars and the planets have been very relevant during these times and that Mother Gaia's vibration has increased out of sight. Who has grown to meet the Son's full strength?

Recently Hermann Müller, the 82-year old Creator and World leader of Psychosomatic Therapy over 25 years passed away. He inspired many thousands to become "one" with the self. A charismatic Indian gentleman possessing a flowing white beard and penetrating eyes, he inspired thousands to become teachers to become candles of light for humanity. At his recent funeral his devoted and beautiful wife Marie carried his Excalibur sword, hilt down (the up side down cross). He passed away at his full ultimate power.

I also have a 2010 guide drawing of a very old man with a white beard and "closed" eyes. I have been guided all along. "Their time is not our time" that continually is reflected in all my writings.

This was like being hit by a lightening bolt- everything twigged. Marie Müller told me that Hermann would have approve of the dedication made to him at the prefix of my story.

On reflection, a significant message came during the time of the 1990's era Croatian crisis, when Riverwood House Bed and Breakfast/Restaurant in Bridgetown was my new home and business.

"Islam troubles the World." Even remembering where I stood when that fell from my mouth. I understood from the Somalia situation that where extremist sects rule, devastation follows to the people and the land.

Considering the conflict still occurs as I write today, religious zealots have become a huge terrorism issue in many countries and traditional cultures now being over-run with millions of middle eastern refugees. I've also considered Russia's leader Putin, or is it the recently elected American Trump?

It has been forecast that there will be no future American president after this election. Is he setting himself up a dynasty, as seen in North Korea?

My angelic messages say that there will be a price to pay for the desecration of Mother Earth, and only time will tell if I am correct about the faces of the men in black and our escape via gossamer wings...

WARNING

One hundred more years for the Glory to come
Who will be there to witness the Glory?

Oh! What becomes of us?

The gentle souls whose lives are pure
will gravitate to a foreign shore
Resplendent in its pure clean air
refreshing all from near and far.

Will Thou accompany me?

Be safe my dear in all Thy do
Remember it's not that hard to do
For should they see the Love in Thee
Then too they feel the Love for Me.

The time of chaos as has been told
Man has worn the cloak too long of
suffering at the hands of few.
Evil takes its toll you see
But those who see Me through you
will be saved in eternity.

The precious Souls of those you Love
Will be wrapped in gossamer fair
Spun with Love from way out here
Here from Sun to Sun.

To make new star seeds so pure and white
Ready to help you all along
Star seeds.

Oh! My Child of Light
What delights my heart so dear?
To see you Care – to see you Love.

That's all I need from you tonight.

Bless your Soul my precious child
For seeking Truth tonight.

It is no coincidence that the 'Ancient Oriental Guide', drawn by energy artist Wendy Ishwe Clarke in 2010, has pride and place in my home. His character reflects in the beautiful rosewood statuette I brought back with me from Singapore in 1964, 'God of Compassion'.

Welcoming all at my front door is a captivating drawing of 'My Lady with the Veil' (Wendy's vision of my half-sister Amandolah from past life experiences in India), again, confirmation of contents of the Darwin Reiki attunements of 2008 and my spiritual relationship to Shanti-A.

The year 2011 brought forth a great rush of work. I believe Vicki Barrett Leonard's guidance had a lot to do with restoring my awareness and the group of twelve sharing similar experiences. Forging 'The Way' through the chaos and distress came questions, guidance and conversations from an angelic source. The time had come to put pen to paper and tell my story.

Blessed with divine guidance, 'Forward - My Walk with the Way' gives credence to what I felt were paranormal events so different to what I had ever experienced before.

It was a time when I had been requested to complete an action by my dearly loved second Mum, Nancy. I was blinded by love for her and capitulated to her request to arrange changes to her personal affairs.

On completion of that task my stomach clenched and nausea rose in a way never felt before. In hind-sight it was a warning of bad karma coming yet she was completely satisfied with the changes. And karma came with accusations and anger out-rightly displayed to me from many quarters. It left me bereft and the following writings flowed.

WHO IS THE KEEPER OF THE SOUL?

Thy thinks Thy knows Thy enemy
But Thoust has the head in the clouds
Love for the Soul and caring for
the Soul overcometh all.

If Thou can match Thy Soul with those of the
angels then Thou should walk with them.

Love of the Soul careth not for worldly riches.
It cares for the safety and the journey to come.

I AM that I AM

And I felt as if I had been persecuted by others.
Still the pen flowed, reflecting on my torment.

THE SOUL LOVER

Thoust does not know in whose camp the enemy lies.

Is it the One who cares for the Soul?

Or, the One who is sustained by fear and anger
that is unleashed in front of the innocent?

The Soul lover protects the innocent
The Soul destroyer thinks only of itself.

NANCY, THE KEEPER OF SECRETS

Who is she that rules my world of folly and foe?
Who is she that giveth Love and
withdraws to see the spill?

Who is she that loves out loud
With joyous tune to call?
Nancy is the lover of them all.

Beware my love for time has come
To answer one and all
Are you the lover of the Heart?
Or the One to come to all?

CONVERSATIONS FROM ABOVE

March 2011. Awoken from a deep sleep, I urgently grabbed the nearest pen. Beautiful, poignant words kept coming, life's instructions. Messages from beyond assisting me through the awful time of self-doubt, where I was at regarding Nancy's requests, unhappy living arrangement and unsatisfactory relationships.

⁓ ⌒ ⌒ ⁓

My dearly loved Nancy had played her hand with many partners. She came through to me after her death, telling me her mind had not been quite right and to let things be.

Nancy had been generous to me throughout her life, being there for the trauma of my still-born daughter Carol, always there during life-threatening emergencies. I loved her personal aroma on her clothes, deep cellular memories of when she cared for me as a toddler after my father died.

Nancy passed over September 2014, a few days short of her 98th birthday, sixty-nine years of love. Upon reflection, it was all there, just ready to be played out. Gratefully, there has been forgiveness, joy and fellowship.

Conversations and guidance, prodding me, asking, "What do you want out of life?"

Some of the messages have such deep meanings. One needs to carefully consider the content, recognize what is being conveyed and then, if required, apply it to one's life.

I AM one of many who has come to guide your Soul. Please feel safe in my care. Your mission has been varied and long and not without stresses and strains. You have given your best as was instructed in The Beginning.

Thou shall come home a free woman who has given all, loved all and accepted all.

Life is not complete without birth and death, like the rising and the setting of the sun. The wind storms and fire of life itself is repeated in human life and so must be accepted. Hardships make the body stronger and the mind resilient.

The calming waters of the God Spring refresh and renew the life force for amazing things.

Keep the eye focused on the Love of man without greed or malice, with a pure heart all things will come as they should.

Be strong in Thy endeavour, be kind and be fair to all you cross. For I AM that I AM in your heart always and will love and protect you from this life to the next.

TRUST IN ME

Trust in ME always for truth shall find the way
Of where your life is going
So do not stray.
Be loving and be guided by Thy own true Love

Always here beside Thee until Thy day to come
Be sure my Love of Thy Findings
For this will be Thy way of sunshine and of Angels.
Is this the final way?

Of sons and daughters always
Thy pain will come again
Be kind and gentle always and soon too Yee will learn
From how Thy can be true.

Follow the heart and let the mind
find its own heart too.
Thou can't be all to everyone
Thy dream is to inspire
Just Love and spread the Word
of all and hence ME too.

Of Love with this world is the finest thing to do.
By loving and adoring the Master up on high
Thou shalt live a life of loving from
within Thy ivory tower.

Be thankful and be giving and then you too shall see
Of the glorious wonders that are there for you and ME
Of goodness and of beauty are there for all to see.

Thy Child of God and Angel light
are blessed as are Thee
My own true Love shall shine in
the darkness and of glee.
Hold the candle high as high can
be for all and Thou to see
Be grateful for the small things that
are there for you and ME.
Shine high, aim high and the Shining can be seen.

Trust Love too hard for all to see
But NEVER enough for ME.
I AM THAT I AM

THY WANDERING STAR

Thy wandering star upon this plane
Oh what is your desire?
To see Thee through the times of old?
Of heart and soul on fire?

What is there then that Thou can see
amongst the murky mire?
Is it enough for you to see it through
And at what cost do you aspire?

My dearest love Thou cannot share
The love of all for you
It comes at great cost to those who care
But freedom at last for you.

My one true love is my only hope-
of salvation through the mire
My Lord on high be with me now
I need you through and through.

Oh! Peaceful one you must aspire
to do what you must do
The angels will guard your way
with brightly shining hue.

Beware the rocks that trip your way
Yet let the sunshine through
Our God of Hosts will always be there
For Yee as millenniums come and go
Oh! Precious child of long ago we
love you through and through.

The following one is particularly relevant to my work and how I endeavour to convey to others to respect their health and the beautiful river of life that lies within.

THE RIVER

The river runs free from shore to shore
Along its merry way
It touches land near and far
To nurture or destroy.

The river forms the heart of man
It weaves to and fro
Taking and giving much
That it may clean and go.

Our blood is like the river
That needs to be clean
Look always for the right things
To make it always gleam.

The river spirit plays for fun
The Soul is always pure
We love it always in this state
But are we so assured?

Chaos ruled my world. I needed to listen. About this time, I began to take a good look at dietary issues and for ways to help.

I had always been an advocate of good, clean and nourishing food. Now again reflecting on The River, what did this tell me? Yes, the pathway had been aligned and all I had to do was follow.

Remnants from a serious childhood health issue had plagued my life. These have been addressed many times, and the emotional and life-long health issues from early childhood are finally being put to rest.

Over the next few years a different approach led to more involvement and education in the raw food movement, and eventually to my becoming very close to Susanna Gornatti. Susanne, a joyous and spontaneous soul whose mission on earth is to heal us through food, is the proprietor of Youth and Joy Raw Food Coaching. I am grateful for the lessons given. Thank you, Earth Angel.

MY LOVE FOR THEE IS LIKE THE WIND

Turbulent, wild untamed thing
That wanders wherein it wants to go
The wind blows strong and spirals out of control.

How then the wind be it so strong
Amongst the clouds so near?
Be it always therein for Yee to see
No – it shall not be.

Ride the wind and ride the waves
Just so you dare
To see what God has made for you
Amongst the jewel seas.
The wind is folly the wind is strong
How do you compare?
Are you like the strong stormy wind
Or the breeze that's barely there?

How long the wind will blow amongst the starry sky
Will nought be gained by you tonight
but thinking will not know

Be blessed my dear in all you do
And to what you aspire
Give love to all you see and do
And create your own wind too.

CHINA

The opportunity presented to travel overseas and learn more of the fascinating country of China, so related to the Reflexology science that had so much impact on my life. I was creating my own wind.

In April 2011, amidst much excitement, I travelled to China as part of a five-person Reflexology study tour. Sarah Moore from Margaret River was my travel companion, along with a friend of many years, Irena Pullin, plus two colleagues from over east – BJ and Bobbie. The following message came just prior to leaving and it still brings joy to my heart.

SUNSHINE IS THERE TO SEE

Sunshine is there to see
For one who flies across the sea
To strengthen views to make one wise
Fly safely there and you will see
The Glory of wonders for you and me.

Oh! Gracious child so fair of face
Be joyous in this period of grace
For yours is all to trace.

I love this piece. Strengthening my views on Reflexology and its 5000 years of history. The amazing country of China and its over seventy different dialects, magnificent culture, the privilege of walking the Great Wall and ringing the great bell situated close to The First Heavenly Gate, and most of all reconnecting with Quan Yin.

This again reverberates on Chinese cultural artefacts I have in my home and visualization experienced in my Darwin Reiki training.

I was grateful to meet up with a colleague recently, who confirmed my past-life role in Ancient China.

Mai Lim told of the balances she made as part of court life. Even her name rings true.

The following was Pam Goodwin's reading for me, "Mai-Lim—This is I, this is you, this is we. In honor and in love we walk together to serve others."

Mai Lim (Marylin)

Lim = man of the trees.

Echoing my love of trees once more and so very much in line with the Ancient Hebrew scripture quotation, "As my ancestors planted me before I was born, so do I plant for those who will come after me.

More of the China adventure is recalled earlier.

TROUBLED WATERS

My beloved sister in law passed away in late April 2011. A loss that is still felt, but with happy memories of a truly generous soul.

Difficulties with family relationships persisted. I felt quite alone even living on the Fairbridge Village site that was full of workers and holiday makers.

I relished the occasions when clients came into my cottage for Reflexology. I was lamenting for more connection and appreciated the time with people I trusted who understood me in that unusual environment.

RETREAT AND DESPAIR

So now retreat? I am down on my luck
But who really cares?
Is this the place through the middle of the stares?
To find my place where nobody cares?

Sons – busy and yet what am I doing here ?
Why have I come?
Do you understand?
What have I become?

Yesterday was like a shining star
Bright as bright could be
It disappeared like the coral under the sea.

Where have I turned to lead me here?
The bleak lonely place beneath the sea
Oh! God forgive me, with my heart so torn.

What will you do to clear away the
pain and no longer fear?
Disappear so nobody can see! And the help came.

LONELY CHILD

Oh! Lonely child of long ago
Where do you wander?
Where do you go so far along in this distant land?
Searching for where to make a stand?

Take my hand and let me guide
You here, there and everywhere.

Take the Word of who I AM
To every part of this land
To show them all that I do care
Of where they are or who they are
Bring their Souls to ME.

For I AM strong among the crowd.

Sing the song of Love for all
So, they listen One and all
That we must be brothers all.

No more fighting — no more wars
What good is that to fight like that
And leave the ground with blood untold.

The ground has seen enough of death
We must live and love again
To reach the place that we call heaven

And be in his arms again.
Don't they know about this place
Surely, they must know again
About the palace here within
That sparkles with diamonds, gold and pearls
That one can hold within their hands?

Diamonds are the precious Love
Gold is for the strength of Bond
And pearls are for the Heart
Many more are here
for those who wish to see
What a casket that would be?

So, ask those whose minds are clear
Do they want to see so pure?
And be content amongst the stars
Of pure delight and ME.
My dearest daughter of land untold
Your bidding now must be
To bring them all home safely
And they all then see ME.

The following came to me after a rather unusual accident during a wedding preparation. It was at the Chapel on the grounds of Fairbridge Village, Pinjarra, where my husband and I lived and worked as part of a team of caretakers.

I was endeavouring to move a wolf spider away from a pew prior to the bride's arrival, however instead of obliging with a shoe lift, the spider ran over my bare foot. I reacted in such a way that my chest very quickly connected with the solid wooden pew.

Others heard the impact from feet away and cringed. A cracked rib and associated discomfort was my companion for some time. Awakening from rest filled with beautiful colour arrived the silver lining.

COLOURS ON SLEEPING

Dear One, my heart is yearning
For more comfortable ways
For the clearing of the old
And for fresh new days.

My heart no longer lingers
Upon the dreamtime phase
It wishes for TRUTH and laughter
To last for the final days.

If love could be found amongst the haze
It truly would be grand
To be valued for what I AM
And not some mental sham.

To put one foot forward in front of the other
And look behind with pride
To achieve and give with LOVE always
Is best by far for all.

To give LOVE to food and be blessed
with that is something sacred too
But one must learn for oneself
Or else be truly spurned.

LOVE comes in many forms
Just be aware of that
And ask your angels every night
Yes! Just chat and chat.

They will hear your call - just wait
And be blessed again - how wonderful is that?

JANUARY 2012

As I am putting words to these passages of Love, I look back and again think of the pertinence of the messages.

It was a time for me when all I wanted to do was to fly away and feel my wings. Frustration at being boxed in. I dreamt of my home far, far away beyond imagination. The sadness reflected in my eyes was palpable.

My daughter experienced intolerable personal difficulties. These words were written in Bunbury at her then home. I had been focusing on the beauty of the trees surrounding the property and I guess these words were meant for her too.

WIND WHISPERING THROUGH THE TREES

Wind whispering through the trees
And sunshine playing on their leaves
Such gentle forces ready to please
To reach out for peace therein.

Oh! Beauty Lord there is within
To touch and feel the joy
That lies within one's heart to feel
When One opens with the key.

The key to life is precious LOVE
That One must expose to all
To live a life that's truly full
Be there for One and all.

So, there my Love your answer's been
Just be and let it be
That joyous heart you seek so far
Is there after all.

Be at peace, be joyous my Love
For you are all but there
Use your wisdom, Love and heart

To bring them all to ME.

IT'S TIME FOR ME TO GO

My time has come that I must go
And prepare the way for ME
For what I AM is more than Thou
And harder for one to see.

The joy has gone from this place
All beautiful to see
I AM needs its space
To grow from its seed.

Its seed has lain so long
In placid waters, deep
Its time has come to spring to life
And flow through for my heart to see.

Thine eyes reflect how I feel
And do not lie to all
The joy has gone in this one place
To fly or not at all.

My heavenly home is far away
So, prepare thyself
To explore time and place
Is the I AM, I AM, I AM of now.

I need to go be by myself
My love of long ago
Bless I AM with precious Love
And kindness thus endow.

Oh! Thank you Lord for you
So, wise and strong for ME
The beauty of the trees and birds
Is peace indeed for ME.

No regrets now - only Love

It's time for me to go.

WHEN LOVE DIES

It is a sad thing to see love die
But with it comes a new perception
Of a blossoming spring and new life.

We cannot hold onto what was once dear
When no life springs from within
What we hope for cannot lie
Because it knows no sin.

In our toil and strife, we cannot see
The measure of our worth
We live as best we can my dear
And dream of far away.

We change our lives as we grow strong
And blessed are Thee too
For you must do what is right for Soul
And leave it up to you.

Present yourself in gracious ways
And bring it to a head.
You have our blessing always now
And as then.

So, be strong, be kind, and good
For we shall meet again
Along the stardust trails we set
When we are born again.

Next time, beware - clear all your doubts
For no more changing ways
We must progress to purist heart
And hurt ourselves no more!

SADNESS

My life is filled with sadness and sorrow
Of what could have been
Strangers comment on it now
So, I must let it go.

To let go and let I AM
Take a measure of my worth
It is not such an easy thing
When One has so much held in worth.

But what is worth?
How is it measured?
Do we seek to apply what others see?
Or what our heart holds dear?
Our hearts are such fragile things
And our body runs asunder
But what I AM in ME
says what I AM is worth
And let no man make ME surrender.

For my Soul deserves to sing its song
As strongly as it can
And then true Joy can spread around
And clear the eyes again.

During this time, I felt like there were two people within me. One that everyone saw (or reality), the other leaving me feeling isolated, yet with a rosy glow within me and wanting nothing but peace.

I knew to keep focused on the heart's desire that eventually things would turn out for the better.

Now is the time of enlightenment. Are you ready – or more precisely – are you willing?

Are you willing to forgo the straps of materialism that affects this world so poorly. Give us your unequivocal love and peace – treat the world as you would treat your Soul – with reverence and care. Let the Sunshine in for the smile is a gift for all humanity. Put grievances aside for they will no longer be effective for those whose smiles light the world.

Bring the light to your eyes – show kindness to all things and peace will be your reward.

Amen

Thank you I AM

TIME TO STOP

There comes a time when one must stop
And look to clear the road
Of sometimes things and heavy loads
That stop the heavenly things.

From moving forward in One's life
Of better, more comfortable being.

Life makes the journey hard
Oh! Why should it be so?
When One loves the son born
And yet to let him go.

If this is what is needed
Then let it go
For living lies is not the way
Be free and let it go.
Lies come from not knowing
Or better yet understanding
That all One wants is precious Love
Not frilled up with candy.

The candy stick will melt away
And leave nothing in its wake
Love has none of that
But there for all the taking
From the River deep
The Soul of the making.

The tears have dried now
There'll be no more
The day will come when they appear
Mourn for ME no more.

But instead rejoice in Love
For this is what I AM
The joy of Love from the Heart

Of I AM, I AM, I AM.

In April 2012, an eagerly awaited family trip to Bali was arranged. Thanks to a cousin, a superb accommodation right on the beach was enjoyed for a full ten days.

I loved being with my daughter, her two children and her friend. One night I awoke at 4.41am and wrote the following at the O-C-N Outrigger, Légion. Within minutes the second one followed on.

BREATH

Breath, so vital to us all
Breath
Or no life at all.

It is what we see and what we fear
That will undo our life so dear
Make every precious moment count
Go out and grab what's there about.

My child of worthy seeking pure
Be sure you Love
Be sure you care.

For breathing now will get you there
Our treasure trove of Love abounds
Reach out my love for all to share.

CHERISH

Our world is changing fast you see
Can you change too and be with ME?
For I AM wonder I AM grand
Here, there and overseas.

Your blessed Love will see ME through
Cherish those for the time will come
When we rise towards the sun.

Do not despair
For hope is there
Toward the rising sun.

Oh! Spirit guide so pure and strong
Will get you there amongst the throng
Of duty, we must all be ONE
To Love I AM amongst the throng.

Oh! Beautiful one be blessed today
For you will see your way today
Be pleased for ME all showing now
The rays of sun so brilliant now.

The maze of wondering what to do?

Joy is for the purist heart
Joy is not to be messed about
And let the sunshine in.

Oh! Joyous one with heart of gold
Be blessed by this ONE of OLD
We can but rise to the call
Bring in those minds or not at all.

Breathe freely now for this will end
On foreign shores
Be blessed again
Thank you I AM.

My elderly mother's 91st birthday in 2012 brought forth a flurry of words that I have dedicated especially to her. I hope 2018 will be a better year for her.

MY SUNSHINE MY LIFE

You sowed the seed a lifetime ago
And gave me precious life
Watched over me with love and care
Till we reached this point.

This point is now a celebration
Of what your life has been
Sunshine - the Sunshine Queen.

Your smile evoked the best in us
And hugs there were a plenty
A guiding hand and listening ear
That would not be tempered.

Your loving arms and ways abound
Will be sorely missed by all
Mothered so sweetly all along
What can we do for you?

We can love the sunshine in your face
And remember what has been
The sunshine now shines higher now
For all the world to see.
Blessed mother
Dearest friend... Gift of God
I love you.

The year 2012 was a clear change from experiencing criminal and non-abiding tenants, to the quietness of preparing our Mount Richon home for our own re-occupation.

Re-painting and renovation work tackled alone was enjoyed but tasking. In the quiet moments around sunset and watching the glorious sun gently bathe the hillside, the words came.

MEMORIES OF LONG AGO

Memories of long ago
Watching the stillness here
Bring back the tide of times gone by
Beneath the yellow sun.

The stillness here
The birds fly freely
The leaves glistening on their limbs
The peaceful quiet fluttering leaf
The stillness here within.

The bird that twitters on the branch
Flittering his wings and doing his dance
The goodness and stillness here within
The dreamtime land once again.

The glory of the bush abounds
The glistening leaves that all abound
The white on brown.

The falling of the leaves
Of purity, what's underneath
The purity of Soul within the trees
Is there for all to see.

The clouds are gathering grey they are
Bringing the rain from far and far
Oh! Glory One the guides of wind
We thank the Lord, once again.

THIS TIME ALONE

Busy hands keep mind at bay
Until the night falls then I say
What do I want from this crazy world?
Do you want to be this way?

I asked my Soul to be very clear
To answer all that I hold dear
To push and shove is not my style
For if I did what would I bear?

My Soul seeks Reverence, Peace and Love
In a gentle land where all must share
A land so lovely, so peaceful and still
To listen to and be guided.

So, what lies ahead, I do not know
Yet why does this sadness flow
Across the dreamtime world so dear?

To be true to one's Soul place
Is not that hard for the human race?
But we strive to be what is not to be
Let's give it up for Grace.

Grace is precious, Grace is clear
For that is what makes our Soul adhere
To that part of us that holds ancient truths
The one part that knows Real Truth.
Truth is Love, Truth is pure

Together in Grace will see us there
In dreamtime land of long ago.
There comes a time when we must bare

The knowledge of long ago
When do we show of what we know?
Who will believe us, who will know
About the Glory yet to come
As we rise towards the sun?

The sun is there for all to see
A brilliant loving core
That showers us with warmth to love
From shore to foreign shore.

She sends her warnings more you see
Do not ignore her or it would be
A sad day for those who do not care
Of Mother Earth's repair.

The Glory of this World is told
In ancient scripts found untold
Journeys we can only dream
Of times of long ago.

Our Mother's Soul is precious Love
That abounds within
Let the glory of our land be found
For the Joy to begin.

We dance with Love, we dance with Joy
For human Love is grand
Let all rejoice in this land
The land of long ago, the dreamtime
land of long ago.

We share the riches from beneath the soil
But do not rape the Soul
The Soul of this precious place
Was meant for Love and care
But do not rape the Soul.

Love the land with all thy Heart
And I will spare you there
For when One Loves with all the Heart
Then we care, we care, we care.

Thank you I AM

In June 2012 restlessness struck again. I was feeling emotionally adrift, yearning for a home a long way from Mother Earth, to where I belonged.

And I was grateful for the support of my guides who kept prodding me through the flowing pen-ship and conversations. They flowed and flowed.

HOME

Home! Home!
Where is home?
Somewhere out there in the night sky?

A place to rest
A place to dream
To dream again by the stream
Of gone by life, of things so clean.

Do you wonder too what might have been?
To see so clearly now
When one looks in?
Oh! Blessed One why do you fear?
We all must come
But clear away that fear.
For this place is heaven sent
Amongst the stars of pure content
So, when you're ready come along
Bring your heart and bring your song.

For you will fly like bluebirds true
Who dally in amongst the hue
Your dreams will take you up you see
You'll see ME there.
I'm free... I'm free.

JOY

The Joy of seeing - what do you feel?
Do you feel strong?
Do you see ME?

My strength lies within these bones
Bones that tell me where I'm from
The distant stars along the way.

Or from the Boon Docks USA
Or from the valleys so green and deep
Or deep-sea washes o'er my feet
Look back and wonder where I AM began.
The joy of seeing begins with ME
ME—the Soul of what I think
ME—the perfect Soul within
ME—who loves the body I'm in.

To please oneself and love so true
To love the ME in ME and you
Brings us closer to Thee you see
Across all worlds, all times, all seas.

We must face our destiny
Be true to I AM
Be True to ME.
The Glory is shed by many now

Oh! Why? Oh! Why? I cry out loud
Do they lose the faith in ME?
What have they done?
They will but see to lose ME now

What folly they play
But I will greet them One by One
The Glory is here to One and all.

My spirit reigns high for those who see
Those Souls who welcome ME
My place reigns high above the stars
Not far - a million miles.

But you can see ME everywhere
In the stars - the clouds - the grass
You can see ME in the waters clear
The flowers - trees - everywhere
My Land - my sea - ME.

Use ME to find you way
Back home where you belong
The loving arms to hold you strong.

My name is FAITH
My name is LOVE.

So, move about amongst the throng
Tell all I AM is there all along
Save those Souls you love so dear
Love them all amongst their fear.

Be glad you have ME close to your heart
Be loved by all be loved in heart
For those who see LOVE in you
Will also come to LOVE ME too.

Then this amazing message arrived:

Oh ! Precious child, with your Love so strong, be ready to meet the throng. Your work has only just begun, be prepared - please be strong. For what I ask for you to do may feel wrong.

I ask of you - please be strong.

My daughter of long ago, your mother here of long ago, has seen and watched you grow and grow. A fragile child to woman strong; so, strong - to walk amongst the throng.

Give Love to all those who seek – Those who can see– Those who can see ME. Your cherished Love is like a cloud. Spread it wide and spread it deep

Use my Words to them inspire,
use the Love for all to see

When you have WON, then you WILL see ME!

Thank you I AM

I reached out again, and the Creator's team answered in truth, to ease my spirit.

When one loses a child from any means it leaves a pain in the heart that never disappears. You may think I'm over it, but no, it is there in your cells of memory that can come fleetingly back in times of despair. We never forget! The Creator wants to keep you too.

CHILD OF HEART AND SPACE

Oh! Lonely child of heart and space
Why do you want to leave this place?
We are here to hold your hand
To fill your heart with Love and Truth
For all to share.

Your journey now will come on strong
Be prepared
For we are ready to launch our song
Amongst those who really care.

Your world is changing - we've said before
That you must go from shore to shore
And follow through the Promise of Old.

Be brave - be true - be sure
For you are own Chosen One
To bring us through, through your eyes
Bring what we treasure and that is Love.

Our wings are preened and shining clean
Gleaming for all those who can see
The Truth of what lies thereabout
It's there deep within your heart.
Share your Love with sisters pure
Those who listen will then be sure
That what you say will come about.

Believe, believe in what we say
For there will come a day

When you too will fly with us
Amongst the stars of pure delight.

And fly with Joy and fly with might
Amongst the heavens - such a sight
We'll wait for you
We know you'll come
Because you've been with us all along.

Praise God - Praise Love
Use all your strength
Show all our Love and your INTENT
It will be hard -it will be long
Be strong - be strong - be strong.

Thank you I AM

MORE CONVERSATION

Oh! My Child of Love and Grace
What can we do tonight?
We can play amongst the stars
And wander to our delight.

We've seen the songs of long ago
Of Truth and beauty that lie within
To tell our past, our lives, our loves
For those who want to know.

The lessons we are here to give
Are sometimes slow to come
Be sure to always write them down
So, others will learn to come.

To come into this phase of mind
Of seeking what is pure
To give your Love to everything
That life provides for sure.

Be patient, be kind to all things
That sometimes drive you mad
Then you can say with all your heart

You won by Heart
You won by Love.

No one can say you didn't try
So, give it your all
To say I love you with your heart
for the Son who sees us all!

My heart is like an open book
That is there for all to see
Be careful of its pages fine
As delicate as can be.

Life treats us all with some despite
Oh! Why I do not know
But we can overcome this flaw
And watch as Love grows strong.

The human Love is so profound
As young pups would know
Why not we love each other so
Those creatures can always show?

They show their Love and Honour
With Loyalty and Trust
How good it would be for us all
If we could do that too.
Love each-other's Soul like that
To Trust and Honour too
To bless each other ONE by ONE
Before the rising sun.

The steps of life are hard for sure
But do not despair
For we are here to hold your hand
and make them disappear.

Trust that we are here to help
To ease along The Way
We watch over you, day and night
Along the life-long trail.

We saw you at your glorious birth
The child that was so unsure
The young at heart
With sad and sorrows
That tore your world apart.

Be blessed my Love for we are here
To watch you as you grow
Into the strong and caring Soul
that you have become.

We now are here to hold your hand
To help others understand
The challenges that are to come
Be strong for them in Heart and Love.

Guide them ONE and all
And watch as Love gives all a chance
To feel the change the Earth will feel
The heaving Soul that hurts within.

Show your Love to heal beyond
The troubles that are to come
Bring them safely through The Gate
of wondrous beautiful things
So, they can play amongst the stars
And to believe again.

Thank you my I AM

And my precious guides who love me for that I AM.

TROUBLES

Troubles, troubles when will they go?
To disappear, or do they come again next year?
We try with all our HEART
To sort our troubles out.

Then why you say
Is it so hard for these to come about?
The time when One seeks Peace
Not to be tempered when the Soul seeks ease.

We strain and strain to do what's right
Right by whom?
Right by might?
We need to look deep within
What does our Soul need?

Ask it please!
Does it need Truth along the way?
Face the day with Truth and Love
And your troubles will fade away.

Bring along the Joy to boot
Face those fears and see them fade
For yesterday has been and gone
And you still have your Love so strong.
Use your Love as your powerful sword
Swathe through that sorrow
For you my child have all you need
I'll be there for you and me
And together we will face tomorrow.

Thank you I AM.

Significant dreams troubled me, especially regarding my only grandson. I continued to question myself with my subconscious help coming to the fore again. Again, the sword appears.

From his birth, I had named my grandson as My Child of Light, a delightful, blonde angel toddler of superb manners.

He developed to be an extremely challenging young man, typical of a star child who couldn't be tamed with traditional schooling and a headache for many. Yet cherished.

Totally fearsome and always willing to go beyond normal limits, my dreams were proving true with the following passage flowing from my pen.

Jacob and his family enjoyed their stays with my husband and I in the very humble abode at Fairbridge Village in Pinjarra, Western Australia, seeking respite during their troubled times.

JACOB

Oh! Child of Golden Light
Where will be you tonight?
Somewhere out there—alone in fright
Or held in tight with ME for might?

The silk cocoon is woven so tight
In fear will break and uncover Thee
Put your faith in ME.

A babe in arms such a delight
With eyes that knew all and Soul that fought
What's brought through for you to fight?

Your life's a struggle that's for sure
But just remember who came fore
That strength inspired us to Love
Is there for all - just unplug
And feel the rain that's yours to grab
And walk in peace again.

Jacob and Sophie's young son Rory, my great-grandson, is a magnificent child. Full of Grace, possessing a most engaging smile, intuitive ears and amazing, deep, knowing eyes. So, it all comes spiraling around. My Child of Light?

On a lighter note, in the winter of 2012 the rose garden in the Mount Richon home was in full bloom, so beautiful.

The following reminds me of the exquisite perfume and the joy I felt. Memories too of the small white leather-backed bible, satin ribbon and a single Papa Meiland red black rose from my wedding day.

THE ROSE

Your petals folding softly out
Your scent brings memories flooding in
Of one red rose and one wedding ring.

Your beauty always to the Love
Colour me always
Pleasure me more.

My strength in Love is there to see
A rose for you
A rose for ME.

One stunning rosebud I held to my nose and to my lips. It brought such a strong feeling of joy and sensuality that brought the words flowing.

MY DELIGHT

Oh! Beauteous one
So, bold and bright
One kiss - one breathe - one delight.

Your short-lived life brings so much Grace
To hold you so
So much in sight
Of what is right, of what is pure.

This Earth's gift for us to share
Oh! Rose of old your Spirit young
Brings joy of Peace and Love
Thank you for your short-lived life
My lovely rose - my delight!

Together with my band of friends we attended two very special evenings with Alison and Graeme Jarrad's magnificent tipi in Sawyers Valley over the last two months of 2012.

The over twenty likeminded souls attending the Conscious Unity event created a crescendo of voices rising through the pitched tipi roof to the flutes, drums and my dream harp strings too. It was amazing.

During the first visit a vision appeared before my eyes of me handing over an open book-like object to a monk-like figure just above me, both of us standing on the highest mountain. I feel the entity encompasses these words of Love for the World.

The following meeting, again with my friends, another vision appeared, yet my voice was heard to say, "I AM the Oracle."

This had a great bearing on my book title. The day after the December 21, 2012, Mayan celebration I fell and badly injured my shoulder. That injury took ten months to heal.

In 2013 I was fortunate enough to support and partake in two intensive psychosomatic healing workshops arranged very early in the year and held in my Mt Richon home over Easter.

Consequential eruptions due to my failure to meet

family expectations of being at an Easter family gathering had unfortunate results.

Psychosomatic Therapy is a practice that aims to align heart and mind to act as one. It provides understanding of how the sub-conscious mind registers changes in the sacred geometry and whole body via distress and/or illness. I needed help as my emotions and body were exhausted. The whole program was extremely challenging and when completed, I felt completely different and stronger.

Later in that year, at the first Tasmanian conference for that international group, I read the following to approximately thirty practitioners. You could have heard a pin drop. Hermann Müller, the grand master of this amazing world-wide group of practitioners, insisted that I continue with the work.

I did so using it as a tool with Reflexology and face reading at the Mandjar Markets in Mandurah, and in some social environments. This following piece clearly shows my sub-conscious state and the heart's desire for my soul and mind to be fully connected.

IN MY MIND, A THOUSAND TIMES

In my mind, a thousand times
I've tried to tell you so
That we - you and me
Are no longer One but Two.

We have both worn the cloak too long
Without the cover of Love and kindness
With wicked words and acts of spite
Does not help One to climb through
The haze of hurt and shame to a better life.

Our young lives have been full of shame
Both for you and me
It's how we move through time to Grace
Is what is needed now.

Yes, you have noticed changes
Within this heart of mine
It's moved from focusing on Thee 100% of time.

To myself, so that I may grow
And live a life that is truly free
Yet still be there for all to see
And perhaps watch you to grow.

Your generous heart is only part of you do see
There is the aspect of self-worth
Is what I fail to see.

You need to focus on yourself
And watch your body clear itself
of those wretched things
That you still hold so near.

We will never tell you what to do
For that is for your Soul's command
Be strong my Love
It takes courage to do it all alone.

But cleansing is what must be done
For us both to live in peace
Be rid of those toxic thoughts
They will only poison the mind
And the body will express it out
Through skin and troubles deep.

Do not look this as a backward step
But one of great desire
To become what is required of us
And be an Enlightened One.

Courage always - chin up high
Be parted best of friends
For when our Souls are clear with light
Then we can love again.

In October 2013, I believe I was answered again with these beautiful words, and my instructions confirmed from many years ago, that I would take a long journey, and to give comfort to those in need.

BLESSINGS

Blessings dear One
Tonight, our Souls are as One
We have fought the mighty battle and have won
Welcome to the throng.

We understand your longing
We understand your Love in time and Grace
Move forward and be the ONE.

Sit quietly now be not in haste
There's lots to learn so do not waste
Your time has come to see them all
To show them now or not at all.

Lead them to us my dear
Be not afraid, have no fear
We are here - always here
Come - join us now.

The following parables came late at night on the 30 October 2015. Please take the time to think about what they say.

Do they speak to you? I know they did as my journey began some twenty years before!

The second piece also strengthens my belief that we are all One Consciousness, to Love and Respect each other always.

TRUTH

At the village gate sat three people. One turned to the another and asked, "Where have I gone wrong in life?"

The others both stared, and remained glum.

The first person then stood and pronounced that he would go searching to find the Truth of who he was, and then set forth on a long journey.

It took many years to find.

There was a time when he sat down again, and asked the same question.

"Where have I gone wrong?"

Then a vision appeared before him and a voice as beautiful as a bevy of angels playing harps of golden music appeared. Enthralled at the sheer beauty he then felt his heart beat out of control and the 'Voice of Infinity' spoke, "Where have you not looked, my son?"

And then, he finally knew after all those years of searching, he had failed to look within.

Thank you I AM.

This is the first of many - always speak well of ME.

Sometimes when a person is feeling low,

all they need do is smile.

This one followed suit.

STRENGTH

There was once a time when a man thought he was the strongest in the land and set out to find another who would give him the opportunity to prove just how strong he was.

No one came.

He became frustrated and began to voice his superiority to others.

No one listened.

Eventually, he stopped on his travels and sat down on the earth, staring at the ground. In his silence of frustration, and feeling his ego totally depleted, his thoughts were distracted by a solitary ant.

The ant then spoke to him and the man gasped in awe.

"Look at me. I am a lonely ant who appears to have lost his way. I AM never alone and my brothers are all surrounding Me. I AM part of them, they are part of Me, and together we are stronger than a man."

Since moving to the sunny, seaside town of Mandurah my life has become further enriched. This is a lovely place to walk my dog Lily, share some joyous times with dear friends and a safe landing for my husband.

The district facilities are excellent for his challenging health issues. We have enjoyed a brief overseas holiday together, and I have continued to spread my wings overseas. I visited amazing China again with a dear friend, relishing family connections in Laos, Phuket and Bali after a four-year absence.

I enjoyed my time in tranquil Tedjakula, Bali where I was guided in meditations and Qi Gong. A flower meditation was led by Dr Daniel Houtman, The Spirit Doctor, with my new-found friends, Rosie, Brigitta and Olga.

I will never forget the explosion that happened in those few moments. The deepest pink spread up my body from my loins, the tears flowed and the 'Voice of Infinity' spoke in Light language. I cried tears for the world.

I appreciated the connection with the local Shaman who concurred how sensitive I was and that in time many will consult with me.

It is my intention to give my utmost to continue the instructions contained in the writings reflected within, and following through my involvement in the

'Find Your Wings Intentions Sanctuary' currently under construction in Brookton, Western Australia. It follows the Ubuntu principle of sharing, caring and building a better life for oneself and others.

I thank all my fellow Light workers, friends and family for without them this would not exist. You all have helped shape my world.

You may ask yourself what have you personally gained from reading this script. Only you can answer that. If by some means a Soul has been freed from restraints of mind behaviour, then the battle has been won. Mine was not an easy road so be prepared -it is worth it in the end.

With the aid of my Spirit Guardians and my love of my own precious Soul Spirit, the foundations of my coming life, experiences and internal conflicts are exposed. May the Spirit be with you all?

My writings have come at times of difficulty with the guiding hand (Soul talk) expressing my true feelings. Yet what still shows through is the love. What are we to bear? What is our worth? Do we continue to give ourselves away and for what? One must trust again those decisions made in the right context of truth.

Some events are revealed in writings that pre-empted events including that of my daughter and grandson. Her trials and life journey have been heart wrenching for me, and I am glad that a successful and meaningful future arrived. I wrote the following words in May 2012.

MY PRECIOUS LITTLE GIRL

I write this from my heart.
You are so troubled - life's not fair
How can you win against the tide?

Be strong in Spirit and in Love
You will find Peace within you there
A place to rest, away from fear
Of what will happen - now or next year.

You share a compassionate life
Of Mother-Daughter am I right?
You want more Love
You want more Life.

Your children Love you I'm not wrong
Remember to listen to them
With full attention to their pleas.

Give thanks to all who care for you
There are so many
Not just a few.

Remember always to show your Love
That brings your beauty to the fore
Love thyself as you must know
Is the only way for I AM to go?

I AM is your Soul uncovered
Bless this night, so it is shared
Along with mine
My daughter is cherished.

I have been blessed to have so many nurturing souls to aid my journey. Fred and Pat Bloomfield, my Mt Richon neighbours, rescued me from an extremely painful event, and ensured an ambulance reached me immediately. Another shoulder encounter that took a long time to heal!

However, out of that event some beautiful writings came forth. I had the opportunity to partake in some amazing workshops in psychosomatics that positively affected my approach to life.

I benefited from raw foods, regeneration healing, and my gratitude for the joy of working under my Power of One with Marylin - Reflexology Sole to Soul gazebo at the Mandjar markets in Mandurah.

The next few years changed my life direction again. New home, unwell family members and to complete my dream of publishing the exquisite profound messages.

My daughter married her great love in September 2016 at Marleston Hill, Bunbury, where they first met. The music for the nuptials was very beautiful. Later that evening and during the casual toasts to the happy couple with family valued friends present, I reminded Catherine about a message received several years ago, just prior to her first face to face meeting with Darren.

I had been at the Mandjar Markets working. After conversing with Shirley Stubbs, medium and fellow stall holder colleague and friend, the words, "turn the page, turn the page" came through. Her new name is Mrs. Page and the music as Catherine walked towards her destiny was "Turn the Page".

There are so many I need to thank for their guidance and love.

My only grandson has yet to clear the way. There came the time that the words 'let go and let God' flowed back into my mind, just as it did for my son many years before. This gave great comfort. Yet I know that my grandson's journey will not be an easy one regardless of his musical talent or the pull of unwelcome influences in this society. Thankfully we experienced a delightful evening together for his 18th birthday, and with trust all things will be well.

His relationship with a very beautiful young woman produced my great grandson Rory, a happy babe with the most beautiful knowing eyes, incredible intuitive ears and engaging smile.

At this very moment, my Spirit remains strong with the intention to maintain true happiness, that is being at One, being at peace with oneself.

For the message received in the year 2001 around the time of the 9/11 disaster in New York, Spirit indicated to me that I needed to go on a long journey. The road remains long and the Spirit remains strong. I will keep my promise to continue to give spiritual comfort to those in need.

The question may arise, "What have you gained from reading this script?"

Only you can answer that. For some it is not an easy road, so be prepared! It is worth it in the end.

Amethyst Starchild

There comes a time
When ONE must stop
And look to clear the road
Of sometimes things and heavy loads
That stop the heavenly things
From moving forward in ONE's life
Of better, more comfortable being.

Life makes the journey hard
Oh! Why should it be so?
When ONE loves, the son born
And yet to let him go
If this is what is needed
Then Let it go.

For living lies is not the way
Be Free and let it go
Lies come from not knowing
Or better yet understanding

That all One wants is precious love
Not frilled up like candy
The candy stick will melt away
And leave nothing in its wake

Love has none of that
But there for all the taking
From the River deep
The Soul of the making!

The tears have dried now
There'll be no more
The day will come when they appear
Mourn for ME no more

But instead, rejoice in Love
For this is what I AM
The joy of Love from the heart
Of I AM, I AM, I AM.

www.ingramcontent.com/pod-product-compliance
Lightning Source LLC
Chambersburg PA
CBHW060434090426
42733CB00011B/2268